Following Jesus
CONTENTS

The Work God Wants (Matthew 10:22; Mark 13:13; John 6:28, 29) 5

Keep the Faith 5

Love with All Your Heart (Matthew 22:35-40; Mark 12:28-34) 6

Be Born Again (John 1:12; 3:1-21; II Corinthians 5:17; Galatians 3:26) 7

My Birth Announcements 8

Join the Family (Matthew 12:46-50; Luke 8:19-21; 11:27, 28; Hebrews 11:6) 9

Get on the Narrow Road (Matthew 7:13, 14) 10

The Old and the New (Matthew 9:16, 17; Mark 2:21, 22; Luke 5:36-39) 11

Build Your House on the Rock (Luke 6:46-49) 12

Love Each Other (John 13:34, 35; 15:17) 13

Tell the Good News (Matthew 9:37, 38; John 4:35-38; Romans 3:23; 5:1, 2) 14

Make a T-Shirt to Help with the Harvest 15

Jesus' Overpaid Workers (Matthew 20:1-16) 16-17

Let Your Light Shine (Matthew 5:14-16) 18

A Bright Reminder 19

Be Salty (Matthew 5:13; Mark 9:50; Luke 14:34) 20

The Prodigal Son (Luke 15:11-24) 21

Help the Poor (Luke 16:19-31) 22

Make Clothespin Puppets 23

The Rich Young Man (Matthew 19:16-26; Mark 10:17-27; Luke 18:18-27) 24

Choose Your Master (Matthew 6:24; Luke 16:13-15; Philippians 4:19) 25

Store Treasure in Heaven (Matthew 6:19-21) 26

Serve God with Money (Matthew 6:25-30; Mark 12:41-44; Luke 12:13-21; 21:1-4;
   Philippians 4:19) 27

Be Sincere (Matthew 16:6-12; 23:24-27; Mark 8:15-21; Luke 12:13; John 1:36) 28

Right Reasons (Luke 12:2, 3) 29

Produce Good Fruit (Matthew 7:15-20; 12:33; Luke 6:43-45; John 15:16;
   Galatians 5:22, 23) 30

Good Ground (Matthew 13:3-8, 18-23; Mark 4:3-8, 14-20; Luke 8:5-8, 11-15) 31
Be Careful Who You Follow (Matthew 7:15; 15:14) 32
Be Sure It's in the Bible (Matthew 15:9; Mark 7:7, 13, 18-23) 33
Remember What's Important (Luke 10:38-42) 34
Daily Planner 35
Keep Your Good Deeds Secret (Matthew 6:1-6, 16-18) 36
Get Rid of What Causes Sin (Matthew 18:7-9; Mark 9:43-47) 37
Count the Cost (Luke 14:28-33) 38
Don't Look Back (Luke 9:57-62) 39
Give God What Is His (Matthew 22:15-22; Mark 12:13-17; Luke 20:19-26) 40
I DID IT! 41
Answers 42-43
Index of Life and Lessons of Jesus Series 44-45
Write the Author 46

Fun Ways to Learn the Whole Story of Jesus and His Love

Following Jesus

Creative Bible-Learning Activities for Children Ages 6-12

The buyer of this book may reproduce pages for classroom or home use.
Duplication for any other use is prohibited without written permission from David C. Cook Publishing Co.

Copyright © 1991 by Tracy Leffingwell Harrast. Published by David C. Cook Publishing Co.
Printed in the United States of America.

All puzzles and Bible activities are based on the NIV.

Scripture taken from the Holy Bible, New International Version, Copyright © 1973,
1978, 1984 International Bible Society.
Used by permission of Zondervan Bible Publishers.

Book Design by Tabb Associates
Cover Illustration by Gary Locke
Interior Illustrations by Anne Kennedy

THIS BOOK BELONGS TO:

_____

To My Children and Others Who Read This Book

Following Jesus makes people happy and prevents many of the problems that sin causes. Will you let Jesus lead every part of your life? He wants you to follow Him because you love Him, not to try to earn your way to heaven. No one can be good enough to deserve living with God. Salvation is His gift to those who have faith in Jesus. If you trust Jesus to save you from your sins and you want to follow Him, please pray right now and ask Him to be your Savior and Lord.

When we believe God has saved us, it shows in the way we live. When we feel how much God loves us, we're able to obey the two greatest commandments—loving Him and those around us. When we disobey, God is loving and forgiving. Don't run away from God, run to Him—He is always waiting for you with His arms open wide.

—Tracy L. Harrast

The Work God Wants

In John 6:28, 29 some people asked Jesus, "What does God want us to do?" These people thought they could gain eternal life by good works. *Decode Jesus' answer to discover the "works" God wants. Below each cross, write the letter that has the same pattern as the cross.*

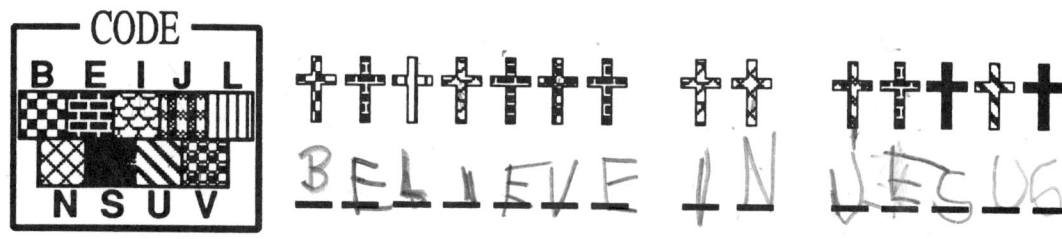

BELIEVE IN JESUS

Keep the Faith

How long does Jesus want us to keep believing in Him? *Fill in the blanks with letters to find what Jesus said in Matthew 10:22 and Mark 13:13. Begin with the letter H after the circle. Write that letter, then skip a letter as you go around the cross. The second time you go around the cross, begin with the letter T that follows the letter H.*

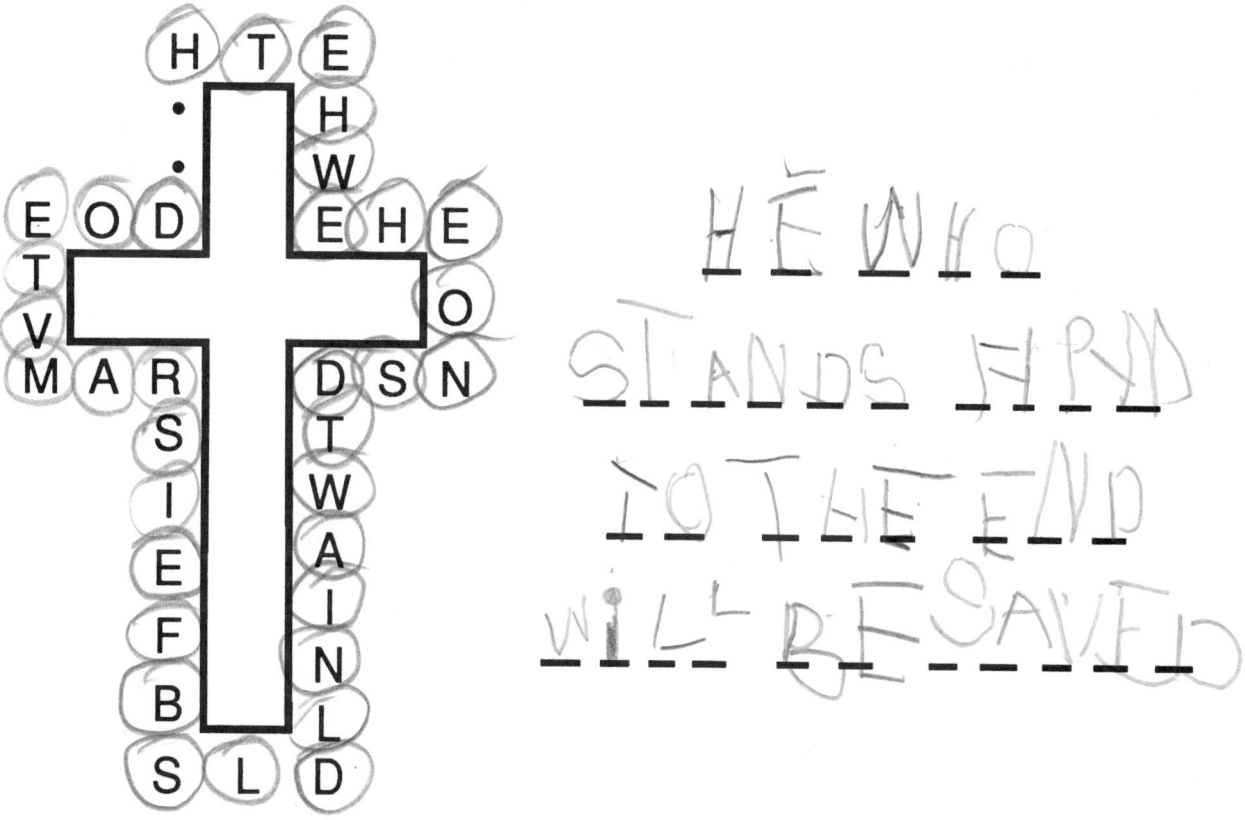

HE WHO STANDS FIRM TO THE END WILL BE SAVED

☐ *Draw a star in this box when you've read Matthew 10:22; Mark 13:13; and John 6:28, 29.*

Love with All Your Heart

Someone once asked Jesus which commandment was the most important. Jesus said to love God will all your heart, soul, mind, and strength. He also said that the second greatest commandment is to love your neighbor as yourself. You can show your love for God as you love others. *Write the names of people you know in these hearts, one name per heart.*

Each day do the following for one of these people:
* *Pray and ask the Lord to take care of the needs that person has. Also ask God to show you what you can do for that person. If he or she doesn't know the Lord, ask God to help you find a good time to talk to the person about Him.*
* *Do kind things for that person, but don't let anyone know about it.*
* *When you find a good time to talk about God, ask that person if he or she has ever trusted Jesus as Savior. If necessary, you can use page 14 to explain how to become a Christian.*

Draw a star in this box when you've read Matthew 22:35-40 and Mark 12:28-34.

Be Born Again

Nicodemus Visits Jesus

In John 3:1-21, a Pharisee named Nicodemus came to Jesus. *Read about his nighttime visit with Jesus and color the pictures.*

Everyone was born once. For our physical bodies that's enough, but God wants each of us to be born again. The second time is when we are born into the family of God and become a new person on the inside. The second birth happens when we trust Jesus to save us from our sins. You can be born again right now. If you'd like, pray a prayer like this in your own words:

Dear God, I want to be born again. I believe Jesus is Your Son and that He died for me so I could be forgiven and could live with You. Please make me the way You want me to be. I'll follow Jesus all of my life. In Jesus' name I pray. Amen.

Draw a star in this box when you've read John 1:12; 3:1-21; II Corinthians 5:17 and Galatians 3:26.

My Birth Announcements

When you were born, your parents probably sent out birth announcements to tell all their friends the good news of your birth! You can fill in the following birth announcements. One for the first time you were born, and the second for when you choose to be born again.

First, fill in the birth announcement of your first birth. If you prayed the prayer on page 7 for the first time today, you are born again. Write today's date on the rebirth announcement. If you have already asked Jesus to be your Lord and Savior, write the day you did that on the rebirth announcement. If you don't remember the day, that's okay—God knows!

Punch holes where there are circles in the cards, and stick paper reinforcements over the holes. Thread pink or blue ribbons through the holes and tie a bow on each announcement.

○ BIRTH ANNOUNCEMENT ○

_____
first name
was born into the
_____
last name
family on
_____
birthdate
in
_____,
city
_____
state

○ RE-BIRTH ANNOUNCEMENT ○

_____
first and last name
was born into the
family of God on
_____
date
in
_____, _____
city   state
when he/she believed
circle one
he/she would be saved
circle one
because of Jesus Christ.

Draw a star in this box when you've read John 3:1-9; II Corinthians 5:17; Galatians 3:26; and John 1:12.

8

Join the Family

Hebrews 11:6 says that you can't please God without faith. When you have faith in Jesus, He helps you do what God wants you to do. When you do God's will, it shows that you have trusted Jesus and are following Him.

One day while Jesus was talking to a crowd, His mother and brothers wanted to speak to Him. When someone told Jesus, He pointed to His followers and said that people who hear God's Word and do it are His family.

A Family Portrait

If you trust Jesus as your Savior and you try to follow Him, draw yourself in this family portrait. Ask your friends or family if they have trusted Jesus as their Savior. If they have, ask them to draw themselves in the picture. If they're not sure, explain how someone can become a member of God's family.

Another time when Jesus was teaching, a woman in the crowd called out, "Your mother is blessed." Jesus said that those who hear the word of God and obey it are blessed (Luke 11:27, 28).

On a separate sheet of paper, write a few things you know God wants you to do. After you do each thing, write beside it how you were blessed by it. For example:

What God would like me to do:
Write to Grandma.
Tell Pam I was sorry.
Tell John about Jesus.

How I was blessed:
She said my letter made her happy.
She forgave me.
I felt great when he became a Christian.

☐ *Draw a star in this box when you've read Matthew 12:46-50; Luke 8:19-21; 11:27, 28; Hebrews 11:6.*

Get on the Narrow Road

When you learn that Jesus can save you, it is like coming to the gate of a road that leads to life forever with God. You can choose whether to get on this road or another. Find what Jesus said about this in Matthew 7:13, 14. *Fill in the missing words and then fit them into the puzzle.*

___ ___ ___ ___ ___ through the narrow ___ ___ ___ ___. For wide is the gate and broad is the road that leads to destruction, and many enter through it. But small is the gate and ___ ___ ___ ___ ___ ___ the road that leads to ___ ___ ___ ___, and only a ___ ___ ___ find it.

Draw a star in this box when you've read Matthew 7:13, 14.

The Old and the New

Jesus told a parable about wine and patches. In New Testament times, people poured wine into wineskins. If they put new wine into an old dry wineskin, it would explode. New wine had to go into new wineskins.

If you got a new pair of jeans, would you cut a piece out of them to patch an old pair? Why not?

What would be wrong with the new pair?
What would be wrong with the old pair?

A Patchwork Puzzle

Each piece of fabric in this quilt has words needed to discover what Jesus was telling people when He talked about wine and patches. Write the word or words in the blank above the correct number.

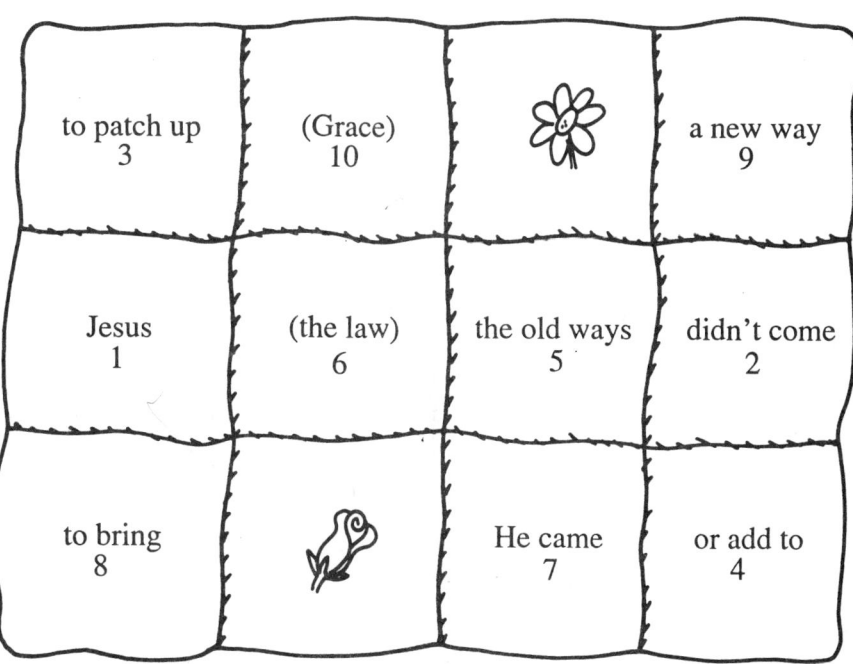

__Jesus__   __didn't come__   __to patch up__
  1   2   3

__or add to__   __the old ways__   __(the law)__
    4   5   6

__He came__   __to bring__   __a new way__   __(Grace)__
    7   8   9   10

☐ *Draw a star in this box when you've read Matthew 9:16, 17; Mark 2:21, 22; Luke 5:36-39.*

Build Your House on the Rock

In Luke 6:46-49, Jesus told a story to show people what a person is like who hears God's Word and practices it. Jesus said, "Whoever comes to Me, hears the things I say and does them will be like a man building a house who dug deep and built the house on a rock. When it stormed and a flood came, the house stood firm because it was well built. But whoever hears and doesn't do what I say is like a man who built his house on the ground without a foundation. The moment the floods came, the house fell and was ruined."

Build a House on the Rock

When you trust Jesus and plan your life on what He says in the Bible, you'll be building your "house" on the "rock."

What You Need

- empty 1/2-gallon milk carton
- scissors
- stapler
- colored paper or fabric
- tape
- tacky glue
- markers
- large, flat rock
- blank piece of paper

What You Do

1. Rinse out the milk carton, staple the top shut, and cut away one side.
2. Decorate the outside to look like a house. Cover it with colored paper. Draw on it with markers.
3. Decorate the inside to look like a house. Glue a carpet scrap or piece of fabric onto the "floor." Cover the "walls" with wallpaper scraps or colored paper. Make miniature furniture from match boxes, pill bottles, and other small objects or glue on pictures of furniture cut from old catalogs. Decorate the "walls" with miniature paintings you've made and a "mirror" cut from foil. Cut out the windows.
4. Write on the roof "My Life." Write on the rock "What Jesus says."
5. Glue the house onto the rock.
6. On a piece of paper, list some of the things you want Jesus to decide in your life and glue this list inside the house.

☐ *Draw a star in this box when you've read Luke 6:46-49.*

Love Each Other

Show You Follow Jesus by Showing Love

Jesus said, "A new command I give you: Love one another. As I have loved you, so you must love one another. By this all men will know that you are my disciples [followers], if you love one another." *Make a card to express your love for others.*

Make an Embossed Card

What You Need
- poster board
- pencil
- sheet of typing paper
- sheet of construction paper
- scissors
- tape

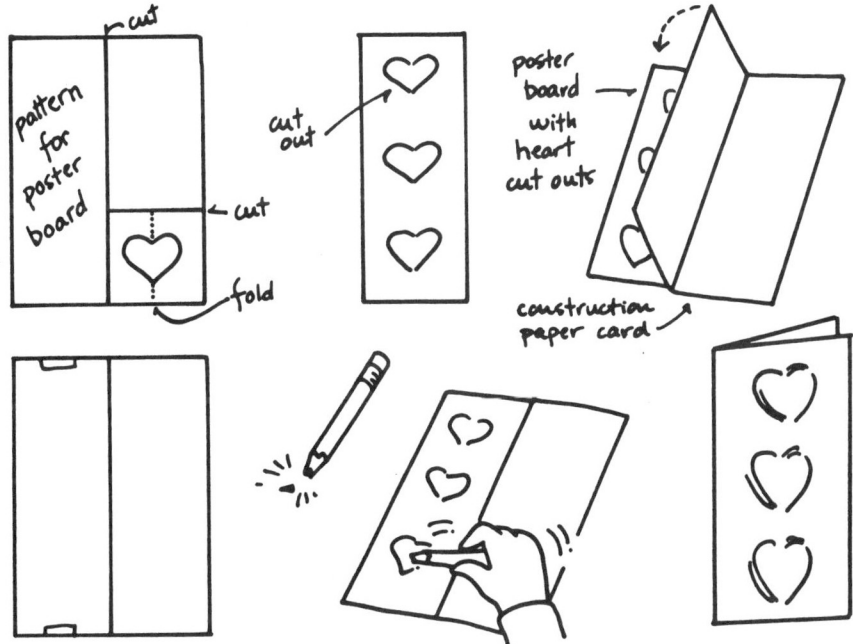

What You Do

1. Fold the typing paper in half lengthwise as shown. Cut along the fold and use half as a pattern to cut a piece of poster board. Cut a heart out of the other half of the sheet of typing paper.

2. Trace three hearts on the poster board piece. Cut the hearts out of the poster board piece.

3. Fold the piece of construction paper in half lengthwise. Lay the left side on top of the piece of poster board that has hearts cut out of it. Tape them together.

4. You'll need to break the lead out of your pencil by pressing it against a scrap piece of paper on a table. Use the pencil without lead to rub across the construction paper until the paper is pressed into the heart cutouts.

5. Very carefully remove the tape.

6. Write a letter inside the construction paper card. It should fit inside a business envelope.

☐ *Draw a star in this box when you've read John 13:34, 35; 15:17.*

Tell the Good News

There's good news and bad news. First, the bad news: everyone sins and that makes us unable to live with God. Now for the good news: God takes our sins away so we can live with Him if we have faith that Jesus died for our sins and was resurrected. Those of us who are forgiven are very thankful to God. Think how glad other people will be when they know that Jesus loves them and will forgive them! He says people are like grain (such as wheat) that is ripe and ready to be harvested (gathered). We should help bring these people to Jesus. We should also pray for God to send more workers to help with the harvest.

Using the words at the bottom of this newspaper, fill in the blanks to complete the Bad News and Good News.

BAD NEWS:

_____ of us deserve to _____ with God because we have all _____.

GOOD NEWS:

If we have _____ in _____, our _____ are _____ and we will live with God.

Word Bank:
sinned, Jesus, None, sins, forgiven, live, faith

Draw a star in this box when you've read John 4:35-38; Matthew 9:37, 38; Romans 3:23; 5:1, 2.

Make a T-Shirt to Help with the Harvest

Wear this T-shirt that announces the good news you have to tell about Jesus. When people ask about your shirt, first explain the bad news, and then tell them the good news. If they want to trust Jesus, offer to pray with them.

What You Need
- pre-washed T-shirt
- cardboard
- pencil
- fabric paint pens

What You Do
1. Put the cardboard inside the shirt to prevent paint from soaking through the front of the shirt and onto the back.
2. Write "I Have Good News" with pencil on the shirt.
3. Trace over the pencil letters with fabric paint pens. If you make mistakes, let them dry. Then trace around each letter with a different color to cover the mistakes.
4. Decorate the shirt however you like.
5. Let the shirt dry before wearing it.

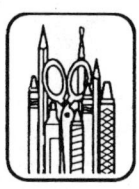

Jesus' Overpaid Workers

Fill in the blanks and read this story Jesus told about workers in the kingdom of God.

The $\underline{k}_{18}$ ingdom of heaven i $\underline{s}_{4}$ like a landowner wh $\underline{o}_{2}$ hired some people to work in his vineyard early one morning. They agreed to be paid a coin called a denarius for the d $\underline{a}_{6}$ y and we $\underline{n}_{13}$ t to work. At different times throughout the $\underline{d}_{3}$ ay, the landowner hired more workers. He told these workers he would pay them whate $\underline{v}_{15}$ er was right.

In the evenin $\underline{g}_{1}$ it $\underline{w}_{17}$ as time to pay the work $\underline{e}_{8}$ rs. $\underline{t}_{11}$ he people hired $\underline{l}_{16}$ ast were paid

Find a Message

Find a message the story teaches by putting the letters that are missing from the numbered blanks of the story into these numbered blanks.

$\overline{1}\ \overline{2}\ \overline{3}\ \overline{4}\ ,\ \overline{1}\ \overline{5}\ \overline{6}\ \overline{7}\ \overline{8}\ \overline{9}\ \overline{4}$

$\overline{10}\ \overline{2}\ \overline{5}\ \overline{8}\ \overline{11}\ \overline{12}\ \overline{6}\ \overline{13}\ \overline{6}\ \overline{13}\ \overline{14}\ \overline{2}\ \overline{13}\ \overline{8}$

$\overline{3}\ \overline{8}\ \overline{4}\ \overline{8}\ \overline{5}\ \overline{15}\ \overline{8}\ \overline{4}\ ,\ \overline{6}\ \overline{13}\ \overline{3}\ \overline{12}\ \overline{8}$

$\overline{1}\ \overline{9}\ \overline{15}\ \overline{8}\ \overline{4}\ \overline{9}\ \overline{11}\ \overline{11}\ \overline{12}\ \overline{8}\ \overline{4}\ \overline{6}\ \overline{10}\ \overline{8}$

$\overline{11}\ \overline{2}\ \overline{6}\ \overline{16}\ \overline{16}\ \overline{17}\ \overline{12}\ \overline{2}\ \overline{8}\ \overline{13}\ \overline{11}\ \overline{8}\ \overline{5}$

$\overline{12}\ \overline{9}\ \overline{4}\ \overline{18}\ \overline{9}\ \overline{13}\ \overline{1}\ \overline{3}\ \overline{2}\ \overline{10}\ .$

first. Eve_r_yone received a denarius _c_oin.
          $\overline{5}$ $\overline{7}$

The ones who worked longest thought they should have been paid more.

The landowner said, "I'm being fair to you. Didn't you agree to work for a denarius? Take your pay and go. I want to pa_y_ the many I
                                      $\overline{14}$

hired the same amount _I_ gave you. Don't I
                                      $\overline{9}$

have the right to do what I want wit_h_ my
                                                              $\overline{12}$

own _m_oney? Are you envious because I am
       $\overline{10}$

generous?

☐ *Draw a star in this box when you've read Matthew 20:1-16.*

Let Your Light Shine

In Matthew 5:14-16, Jesus said, "You are the light of the world. A city on a hill cannot be hidden. Neither do people light a lamp and put it under a bowl. Instead they put it on its stand, and it gives light to everyone in the house. In the same way, let your light shine before men, that they may see your good deeds and praise your Father in heaven."

A Bright Idea Puzzle

Find each picture's word in the puzzle and color those letters yellow. Fill in the remaining letters with a black pen to find a bright idea.

```
STARBRIGHTENLAMP
TORCHTHESUNWORLD
AROUNDFLASHLIGHT
LIGHTBULBYOULANTERN
BYCANDLELETTINGCAMPFIRE
PEOPLELIGHTNINGSEE
JESUSLIGHTHOUSEIN
FIREWORKSYOU
```

Draw a star in this box when you've read Matthew 5:14-16.

A Bright Reminder

You can let your light shine for Jesus wherever you are. *Make this candleholder to remind you to shine brightly for Jesus.*

What You Need

- a clean jar (baby food jars work well)
- ruler
- construction paper
- scissors
- tape
- pencil
- pushpin
- newspaper
- a votive candle or other small candle

What You Do

1. Measure the width and height of the jar. Cut a strip of construction paper that will cover the jar.
2. Write "I will let my light shine" in simple letters on the construction paper strip. Lay it on newspaper.
3. Poke evenly spaced holes in the letters.
4. Tape the strip around the OUTSIDE of the jar.
5. Place the candle inside the jar.
6. When you burn the candle, remember to let Jesus' light shine in you.

Unscramble these ways to let your light shine.

VIEG A GIB LIMES

_____

LETL TOBUA SEUJS

Tell about Jesus

_____

FEOFR OT PHLE OPELRE

_____

OFGREIV TOHRES

_____

A City on a Hill

Find a postcard of a big city. Use a straight pin to poke holes where there are windows in buildings. Hold a flashlight behind the postcard in the dark to see what the city would look like at night.

Be Salty

In Matthew 5:13, Jesus said, "You are the salt of the earth. But if the salt loses its saltiness, how can it be made salty again? It is no longer good for anything, except to be thrown out and trampled by men."

Serve salted and unsalted popcorn to your family or friends. Can they tell a difference? Jesus doesn't want you to just blend in with everyone else in the world. He wants you to make a noticeable difference like salt makes a noticeable difference in food. If you tell people they can be saved through faith in Jesus, that makes their lives better the way salt makes food taste better.

Salt Picture

Make a colored salt picture to remind you that Jesus wants His followers to be the salt of the earth—and make a difference for Him.

What You Need
- salt
- paper cups
- food coloring
- paper plate
- pencil
- newspaper
- glue

To make colored salt: You'll need one paper cup for each color. Fill each paper cup about 1/4 full of salt. Add one drop of food coloring. Stir well.

What You Do
1. Draw your face on a paper plate and write "I am the salt of the earth" beneath it.
2. Trace a section of the picture lightly with glue and sprinkle on colored salt. Shake off the extra colored salt onto a piece of newspaper. Add more glue and colored salt until the plate is covered.

Draw a star in the box when you've read Matthew 5:13; Mark 9:50; Luke 14:34.

The Prodigal Son

In Luke 15:11-24, Jesus told a great parable that some people call "The Prodigal Son." The parable goes like this. A man had two sons. One day the younger son asked his father for the money he was supposed to get after his father died. The father gave the money to him.

Soon after that the younger son left home with everything he had and went far away. The son wasted his money and when it was all gone, he needed to find a job. The only work he could get was feeding pigs for a farmer. He was so poor and hungry that even the pig's food looked good to him. He thought, "Why am I starving when my father's servants have plenty to eat? Even though I don't deserve to be called his son anymore, I'm going home and will beg my father to let me work for him."

When the father saw the son coming, he ran to welcome his son. The father kissed him, hugged him, and gave him clothes. Then the father had his servants prepare a special dinner to celebrate the return of his son.

Sometimes we're like the son in the story. We run away from God and do things our own way. Even though we long to go back to God, we're afraid He will be angry. God is like the father in the story. He will welcome us back and forgive us. That's how much God loves us.

Help the Son Get Back to His Father

Draw a star in this box when you've read Luke 15:11-24.

Help the Poor

In Luke 16:19-31, Jesus told a story to warn the wealthy about being selfish and trusting their wealth instead of Him.

Read the story and complete the puzzle with the missing words.

A rich man wore fancy _____ (5-down) and lived in luxury every day. A poor _____ (3-down) named Lazarus laid at the rich man's gate longing to eat the scraps that fell from the rich man's _____ (6-across). Lazarus was covered with sores, which the dogs licked.

Both men _____ (4-across). The angels carried Lazarus to be with the prophet Abraham. The rich man was buried and went to hell. While he was suffering there, he saw Abraham and Lazarus far way. He called out to say to Abraham, "Feel sorry for me. Send Lazarus to dip the tip of his finger in _____ (2-across) and cool my tongue, because I am in agony in this fire."

Abraham said, "Remember that in your lifetime you received good things while Lazarus received bad things, but now he is comforted here and you are in agony. Also, a big hole has been made between us so no one can go from here to there or from there to here."

The man who had been rich said, "Then please send Lazarus to _____ (2-down) my five brothers so they won't also come to this place of torment."

Abraham said, "They have the words of the _____ (7-across) [in the Bible]. If they won't listen [to what is in the Bible], they won't believe even if someone rose from the _____ (1-down)."

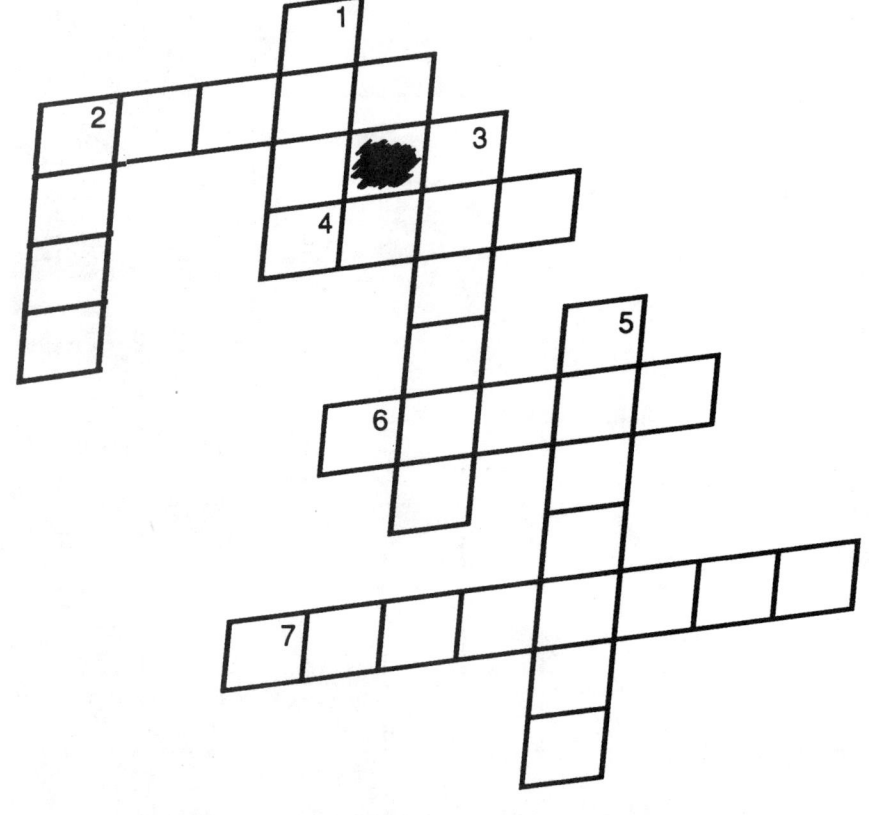

Draw a star in this box when you've read Luke 16:19-31.

22

Make Clothespin Puppets

Use these clothespin puppets to act out the story Jesus told about Lazarus and the rich man.

What You Need

- 3 clothespins
- markers
- small pieces of colorful fabrics
- small pieces of brown fabric
- small pieces of white fabric
- twine
- glue
- scissors

What You Do

1. Using the markers, draw a face on each of the three clothespins.
2. Cut out a piece of colorful fabric and wrap around one of the clothespin puppets. Tie twine around the middle for a belt. This is the rich man.
3. Cut out a piece of brown fabric, wrap around one of the clothespins, and tie in the middle with a piece of twine. This is Lazarus.
4. Cut out a piece of white fabric, wrap around the last of the clothespins, and tie a piece of twine around the middle. This is Abraham.
5. Pieces of fabric can be cut out and glued to the heads of the puppets if you'd like.
6. Act out the story of the rich man and Lazarus.

The Rich Young Man

Figure out this word picture puzzle to read about the conversation Jesus had with a rich young man.

A 🏚+thy young 👦 had tried all of his life 2 do what was ⬅➡.

When he asked 🧔 how he could have eternal life, 🧔 said 4 him 2 sell everything he owned, 2 give the $ 2 the poor, & 2 follow 🧔. The young 👦 went away ☹ 🐝+ cause he was very 🏚+thy.

🧔 said, "It is easier 4 a 🐪 2 🚦 through the 👁 (hole) of A 🪡 than 4 A 🏚+thy 👦 2 🚦 N+2 the 👑+dom of God."

Find the Promise

Color the shapes that do not have dollar or cent signs in them.

If you agree with the promise, sign your name here.

Signed, _____

☐ *Draw a star in this box when you've read Matthew 19:16-26; Mark 10:17-27; Luke 18:18-27.*

24

Choose Your Master

Even though you don't have a job yet, it's important to decide now whether you'll spend your life trying to get rich or trying to follow God. In Matthew 6:24 and Luke 16:13-15, Jesus said you can't do both. You have to make a choice.

Who Will Be Your Master?
Circle one.

Use this code to find out what Jesus said.

A = ①　　M =

G = ㉕　　Y =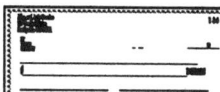

O = ◉　　E = ⑩

D = ⑤　　N =

"YOU CANNOT SERVE BOTH

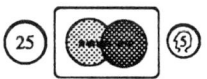   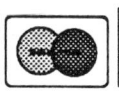  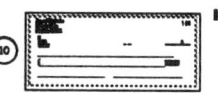

<u>G</u> <u>O</u> <u>D</u>　<u>A</u> <u>N</u> <u>D</u>　<u>M</u> <u>O</u> <u>N</u> <u>E</u> <u>Y</u>."

What Do You Want to Be When You Grow Up?

What will you be someday? A police officer? A homemaker? An undercover agent? Be sure to ask God to help you choose your career because you'll probably spend most of your time working. Will you be working just for money or will you be serving God by helping people through what you do? *Draw yourself doing the job you think God might want you to do.*

 Draw a star in this box when you've read Matthew 6:24; Luke 16:13-15; Philippians 4:19.

Store Treasure in Heaven

In Matthew 6:19-21, Jesus talked about storing up treasure in heaven. He wanted His followers to think about and care for things that will last forever. *Use a pencil to write on this treasure chest what you think and care about the most.* Will your "treasures" last forever?

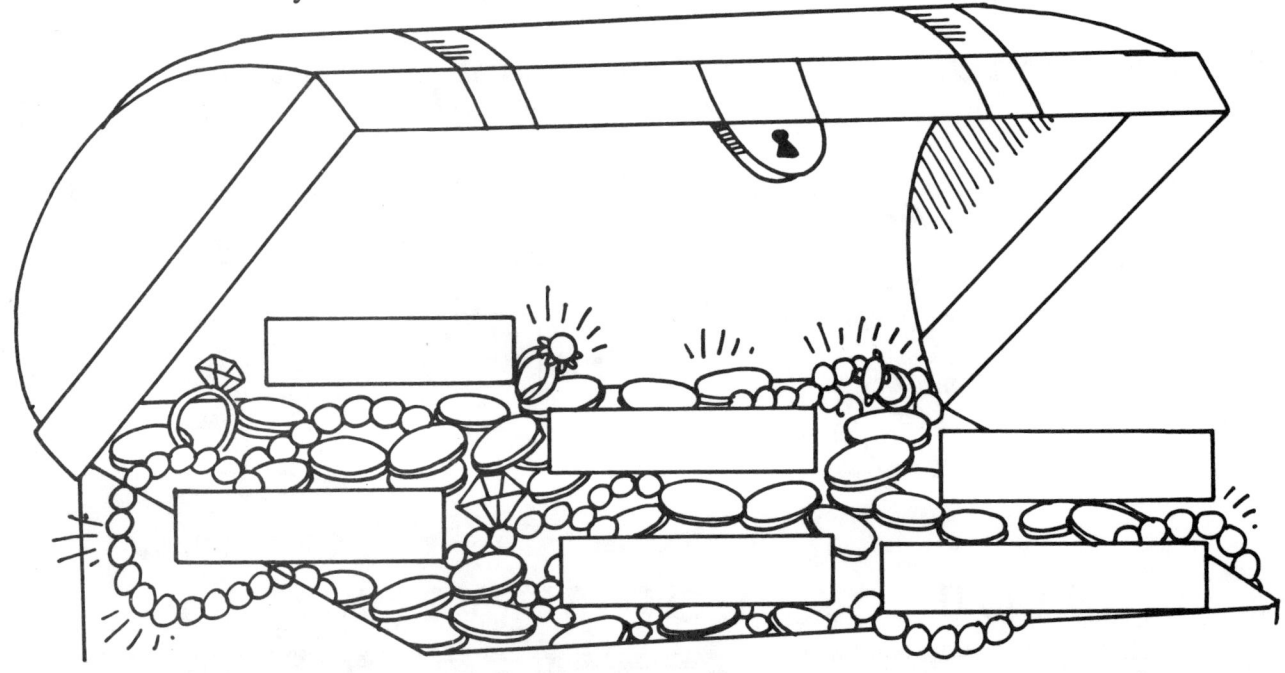

Next, erase things that could fall apart, wear out, or get stolen. Jesus said not to treasure things like that. Instead, He wants us to store up treasure in heaven—what we will care about when we get to heaven. *Write these things in the empty spaces.*

Why did Jesus tell us to store treasure in heaven? *To find Jesus' reason, cross out the letters that spell the picture beside the word.*

Y A U O T O M O U B I R L E
M H O E N A E R Y T
W H O I U L S L E
B J E E W E L R Y
W B H O A E T R E
T E L Y E O V U I R S I O N
T C R L O E T A H S E U S R E
I T S O Y S

☐ *Draw a star in this box when you've read Matthew 6:19-21.*

26

Serve God with Money

We can trust God to provide everything we need. He also wants us to use everything in our lives to serve Him, including our money. Jesus often warned that riches could get between people and their relationships with God. He said your life isn't made of things you own.

One day Jesus saw a poor widow give two small coins as her offering at the temple. Jesus said she had given more than everyone else because it was all she had to live on. She had learned to trust God to take care of her needs.

Using Money the Right Way

When God blesses you with money, be sure that you don't let it come between you and the Lord. Always use money the way God wants you to use it. *Unscramble these ways money can cause some people problems.*

MEOS EFEL HEYT OD TNO DEEN GDO.

_____

MESO TKHIN EYHT REA TERTEB HANT THERO EPOLEP.

_____

MESO LLIW TON RESHA THWI OHERTS.

_____

SMOE OD TON TEL DGO SEU HERIT NOMEY WOH EH STNAW.

_____

List ways you can serve God with money:

_____
_____

☐ *Draw a star in this box when you've read Matthew 6:25-30; Mark 12:41-44; Luke 12:13-21, 21:1-4; Philippians 4:19.*

Be Sincere

Jesus often scolded some religious leaders for being hypocrites. A hypocrite is someone who pretends to be one thing, but really is another. The religious leaders pretended to love and serve God, when they were really looking out for themselves. These religious leaders said and did all the right things, but for all the wrong reasons. Jesus said the hypocrisy of these leaders was like yeast in bread. Yeast quickly affects the entire loaf of bread. Hypocrisy is the same way. It can spread among people and have a negative influence. Jesus compared hypocrisy to other things, too.

Gnats and Camels

Jesus said that the hypocrites strained their water to keep from swallowing a gnat, but then they swallowed a camel. *Cross out the camels with one hump to find out what He meant.*

(Camels spell out: YOU ~~EAT~~ OBEY ~~PICKY~~ LITTLE ~~BIG~~ LAWS BUT ~~OR~~ DISOBEY GOD IN ~~ON~~ BIG ~~LITTLE~~ WAYS)

Dirty Dishes

Jesus said that the hypocrites cleaned the outside of the cup and dish, but left the inside filthy. He said they should have cleaned the inside of the cup and dish first and then the outside would also be clean. *Cross out the dirty cups to find what Jesus meant.*

(Cups spell out: DON'T TO BE TRULY ~~SEEM~~ GOOD ~~BAD~~ PEOPLE MUST ~~OUTSIDE~~ HAVE ~~OR~~ THEIR HEARTS ~~DIRTY~~ CHANGED ~~BAD~~ BY ~~INSIDE~~ JESUS)

Pretty Tombs Full of Dead Bones

Jesus told the hypocrites, "You are like white-washed tombs, which look beautiful on the outside but on the inside are full of dead men's bones." *To find out why they were like tombs, color in the bones that have a dot on them.*

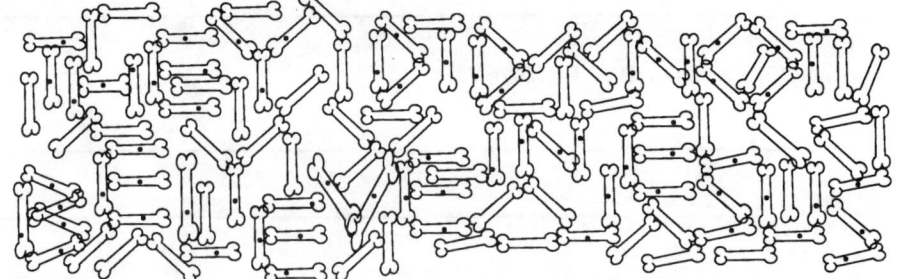

Draw a star in this box when you've read Matthew 16:6-12; 23:24-27; Mark 8:15-21; Luke 12:13; John 1:36.

Right Reasons

In Luke 12:2, 3, Jesus had a warning to people who have secret wrong reasons for what they do and say. *Put the first letter of each word at the end of the word to find out what Jesus said.*

ganythin uyo ehid lwil eb nshow rlate. twha uyo ysa

_____

ni eth kdar lwil eb dhear ni eth tdayligh. twha uyo

_____

rwhispe ni ryou mroo lwil eb dyelle mfro eth froo.

_____

What Are the Right Reasons?

Each picture shows a kid doing something good for the wrong reason. *Cross out what each kid is saying or thinking. Then, below each picture, write a good reason instead.*

"I'm going to shovel Miss Edington's sidewalk. She'll think I'm a nice kid and maybe pay me $5.00."

"Maybe Mom will be so glad I'm cleaning my room that she'll buy me the cassette I want."

"I hope all the kids see how much money I'm giving. They'll think I'm really great."

☐ *Draw a star in this box when you've read Luke 12:2, 3.*

Produce Good Fruit

Good trees produce fruit that is good for people. Trees that are rotten and have gone bad produce fruit that isn't good for people. Jesus said people are like trees. Our attitudes and actions show what kind of people we are. If we're good people, we produce good "fruit."

Jesus said to watch out for leaders who aren't good. He said you can tell whether to follow them by watching what they say and do–"By their fruit you will know them." Jesus wants all of us to produce good fruit.

Fruit of the Spirit

Galatians 5:22, 23 says the Holy Spirit will help God's people to grow these kinds of "fruit" in their lives: love, joy, peace, patience, kindness, goodness, faithfulness, gentleness, and self-control. *Find a trait in each piece of fruit. The letters go in all directions. The first one is done for you.*

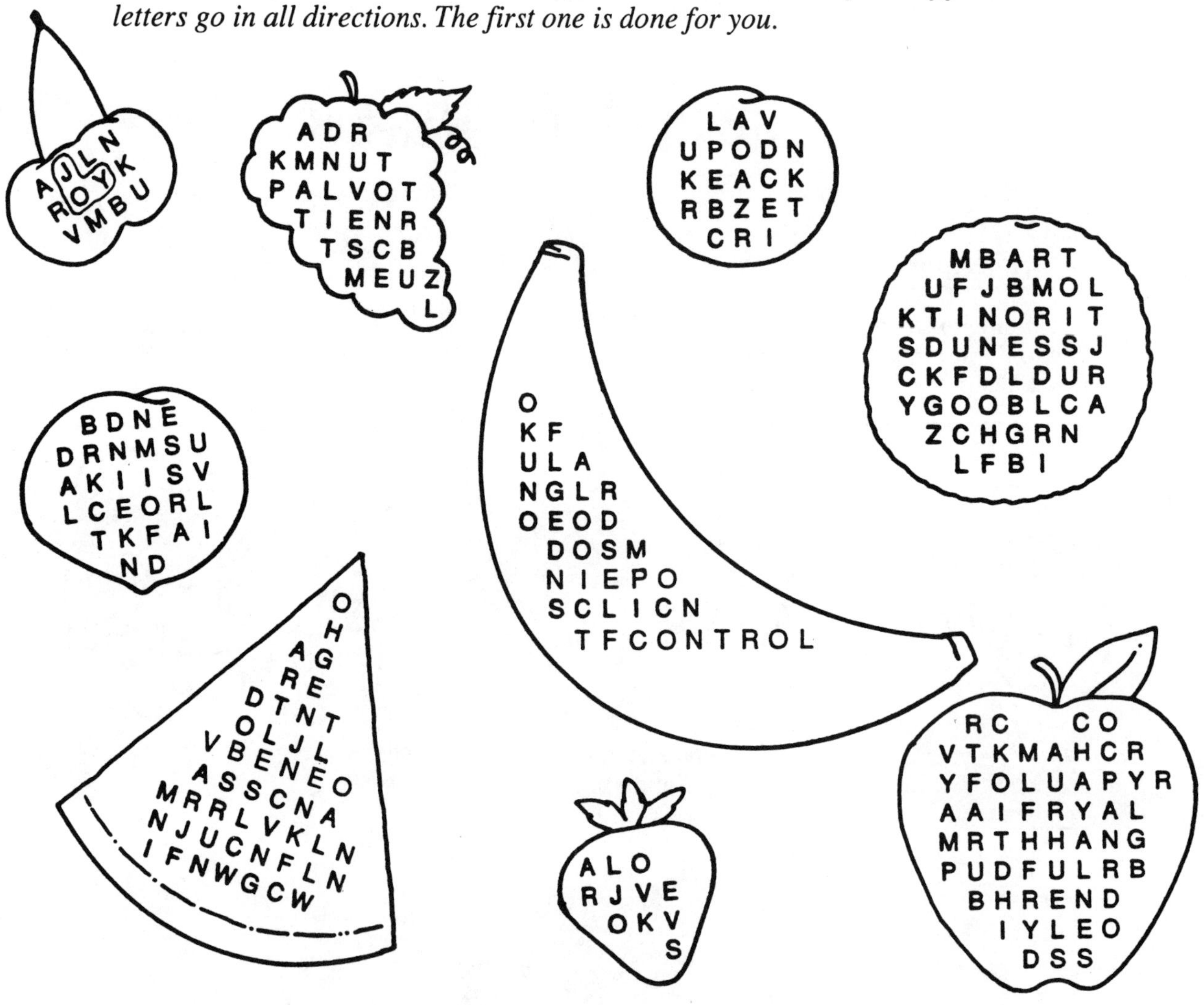

☐ *Draw a star in this box when you've read Matthew 7:15-20; 12:33; Luke 6:43-45; John 15:16; and Galatians 5:22, 23.*

Good Ground

Jesus once told a story about a farmer who sowed some seeds. In Bible times, a farmer would usually hold a bag of grain or other seeds and throw them onto the soil. In Jesus' story the seeds landed in these four places.

1. By a path and birds ate them.

2. On rocky places. They sprouted up quickly but shriveled because they didn't have roots.

3. Among thorns, which choked them and kept them from producing fruit.

4. On good ground and produced lots of fruit.

Jesus explained that this is like what happens when people hear the Word of God. If a person believes in Jesus and welcomes Him into his or her life, that person's faith will grow and take root—that person will serve God. But sometimes other things keep a person's faith from taking root. *Match the people to the pictures and put the correct number in each box. If you need help, look in Matthew 13:18-23.*

A☐ B☐ C☐ D☐

Which kind of ground are you? Write the number here: _____.

☐ *Draw a star in this box when you've read Matthew 13:3-8, 18-23; Mark 4:3-8, 14-20; and Luke 8:5-8, 11-15.*

Be Careful Who You Follow

Some people who are leaders don't really know Jesus. They try to lead other people when they don't know where they're going themselves. *Use the Braille code to find out what Jesus says about this in Matthew 7:15 and 15:14.*

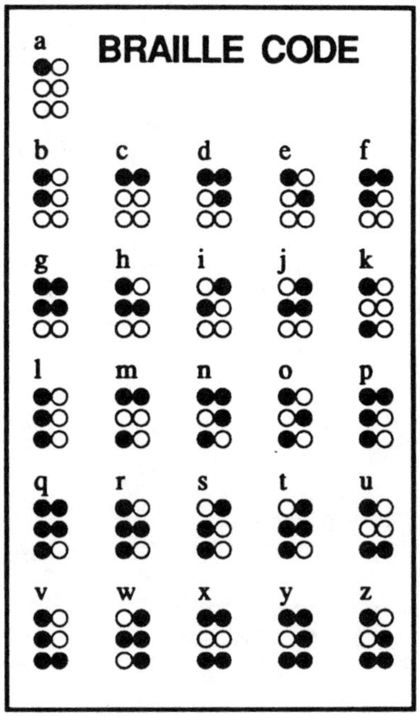

BRAILLE CODE

Matt. 15:14

Make a Wolf-in-Sheep Puppet

Jesus said to watch out for some people who pretend to be sheep following Jesus, the Good Shepherd, but who are really like wolves on the inside, waiting to harm the sheep.

What You Need
- 2 disposable cups
- scissors
- cotton balls
- glue
- permanent markers
- scraps of brown felt or paper
- tape

What You Do
1. Cut a large hole as shown in the cup used for the sheep. Glue cotton balls all over the cup.
2. Insert the wolf cup inside the sheep cup. Draw a wolf face on the cup as shown. Pull out the wolf cup, cut small triangles for ears, and tape the ears to the wolf as shown.

Draw a star in this box when you've read Matthew 7:15; 15:14.

Be Sure It's in the Bible

Jesus said that some people make up rules and treat these rules as if they're God's commands. These rules can get in the way of a person doing what is right. Some people think that keeping extra rules about how you live or what you eat or drink makes you a good person. Some of these rules are good advice, but they are not commandments from God. Jesus said that obeying these rules isn't what makes a person good, but what comes out of a person's heart does.

Always be sure the things you believe are really found in the Bible. When you want to learn about a certain topic, such as "faith" or "love" in the Bible, you can look it up in a *concordance*. A concordance tells you which Bible verses use that specific word.

Is It in the Bible?

A concordance is a great tool to help you find things in the Bible. Words are listed in alphabetical order. When you find the word you are looking for, you will see a list of Bible passages that have used the word in them. *Use a concordance to find out which of these animals are mentioned in the Bible. If you have never used a concordance before, ask a grown-up to help you.*

YES NO	YES NO	YES NO
YES NO	YES NO	YES NO

Draw a star in this box when you've read Matthew 15:9; Mark 7:7, 13, 18-23.

Remember What's Important

Mary and Martha

Jesus went to visit two sisters named Mary and Martha. Mary sat at Jesus' feet and listened to Him. But Martha was very busy preparing for their guest. Martha asked Jesus, "Lord, don't You care that my sister isn't helping me serve? Tell her to help me." Jesus said, "Martha, you are too careful and worried about many things. Only one thing is needed. Mary has chosen that. It won't be taken away from her."

Decode What Martha Learned

🔪 = A   🥧 = F   🥣 = N   🥖 = T

🥄 = B   🥄 = H   ☕ = O   🧤 = U

🥘 = D   🫕 = L   🧺 = R   🧱 = Y

🍷 = E   🫙 = M   🔪 = S

MESSAGE:

DO NOT BE TOO BUSY TO LEARN FROM THE LORD.

☐ *Draw a star when you've read Luke 10:38-42.*

DAILY PLANNER

Spending time with God is one of the most important things you can do. *Write in when you will pray and study the Bible each day. Then fill in your other activities.*

	SUN	MON	TUE	WED	THU	FRI	SAT
7:00							
7:30							
8:00							
8:30							
9:00							
9:30							
10:00							
10:30							
11:00							
11:30							
NOON							
12:30							
1:00							
1:30							
2:00							
2:30							
3:00							
3:30							
4:00							
4:30							
5:00							
5:30							
6:00							
6:30							
7:00							
7:30							
8:00							
8:30							
9:00							

Keep Your Good Deeds Secret

Jesus said not to do good deeds in front of people to try to make them think you are good. If you do, you won't be rewarded by your Father in heaven. Don't tell people when you give to the needy. People who do that have already received their reward. Jesus said not to even let your left hand know what your right hand is doing. Do good things secretly and God will reward you openly.

Make Handprint Pictures

To remind you not to let your left hand know what your right hand is doing, trace your hands on other sheets of paper and then add details to make these pictures.

Draw a star in this box when you've read Matthew 6:1-6, 16-18.

Get Rid of What Causes Sin

Jesus wants us to do what's right. He said we should get rid of what causes us to do wrong things. In fact, Jesus said that we would be better off without our hands, feet, or eyes than for us to let them cause us to sin. Now, He didn't mean we should actually get rid of our hands, feet, and eyes. He was pointing out that sometimes there are things that we <u>think</u> are necessary, but if they cause us to sin, they aren't really necessary and we should get rid of them.

Put the initial from each ring in the blanks with the same number as the hand wearing the ring. You will discover some things that may cause you to do wrong things.

$\underline{T}_4 \ \underline{E}_1 \ \underline{L}_5 \ \underline{E}_1 \ \underline{V}_7 \ \underline{I}_6 \ \underline{S}_8 \ \underline{I}_6 \ \underline{O}_9 \ \underline{N}_{10}$

How might this cause you to sin?

$\underline{F}_2 \ \underline{R}_{13} \ \underline{I}_6 \ \underline{E}_1 \ \underline{N}_{10} \ \underline{D}_3 \ \underline{S}_8$

How might this cause you to sin?

$\underline{M}_{11} \ \underline{O}_9 \ \underline{N}_{10} \ \underline{E}_1 \ \underline{Y}_{12}$

How might this cause you to sin?

Can you think of other things that may seem necessary, but actually could cause you to sin?

_____

Draw a star in this box when you've read Matthew 18:7-9 and Mark 9:43-47.

Count the Cost

A Man Building a Tower

In Luke 14:28-33, Jesus asked some questions. "Doesn't a man building a tower figure out how much it will cost before he begins? Otherwise people will make fun of him when they see he wasn't able to finish what he started."

A King Going to Battle

Jesus also asked, "Doesn't a king fighting a war against another king figure out whether he has enough men to win? If he doesn't have enough, he will ask the other king what he wants so they can prevent a war."

Someone Wanting to Follow Jesus

Jesus said, "In the same way, any of you who does not give up everything he has cannot be my disciple." To become Jesus' followers, we must trust our very lives to Him. Will we give Him all of our time? Will we use all of our money the way He wants? Will we be willing to do whatever He asks?

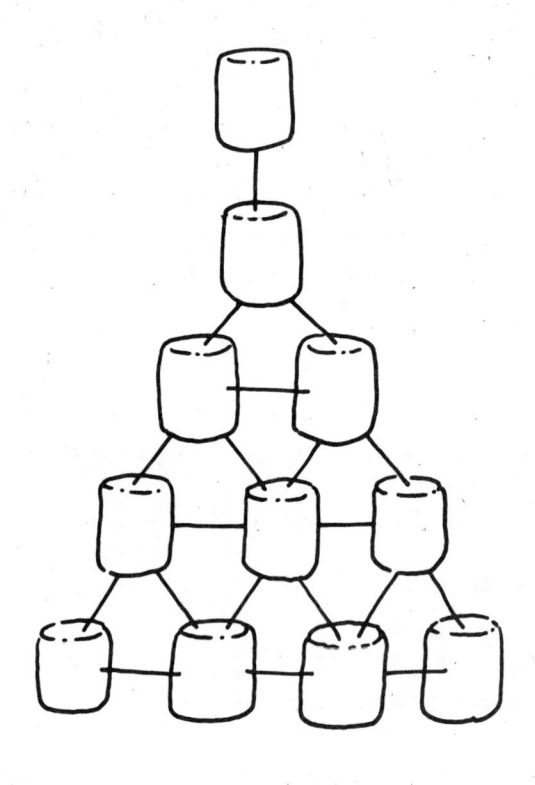

Build this tower with marshmallows & toothpicks. Before you begin, count how many marshmallows and toothpicks you will need. Check the number in the answers on page 43. Have you thought about what it will take to follow Jesus? Will you trust Him with everything in your life?

Draw a star in this box when you're read Luke 14:28-33.

Don't Look Back

One day when Jesus asked some people to follow Him, all had reasons why they couldn't go right then. Jesus said that no one who puts his hand to the plow and looks back is ready to serve Him. Plowing breaks up hard soil to make it easier for a seed to get in and grow. Jesus wants us to love others like He does; this softens their hard hearts so they are ready to receive Him as Lord and Savior.

Plow on Paper

A plow makes straight rows in a field like lines on notebook paper. *Pretend your pen is a plow and trace the lines on this page. Halfway across each line, look over your shoulder and keep drawing. What happens?* If you keep going while looking back, you do a poor job. If you stop while looking back, the work doesn't get done.

Decode this message by changing every A to E, every E to A, every I to O, and every O to I.

Dacoda ti sarva Jasus end than din't sliw diwn ir stip.

Decide to serve Jesus AND then don't slow down

Din't avar thonk ebiut giong beck ti tha lofa yiu hed

or stop

bafira yiu eskad Jasus ti ba yiur Lird.

Draw a star in this box when you've read Luke 9:57-62.

Give God What Is His

Some people asked Jesus if they should pay money to the Roman leader, Caesar. Jesus told them to show Him a coin used to pay the tax to Rome. When they brought Jesus a coin called a denarius, He asked whose image and name was on the coin. They said, "Caesar's." Jesus said, "Give to Caesar what is Caesar's and to God what is God's."

1. The denarius coin was made with Caesar's image on it. Who was made in God's image? (Gen. 1:27)

_____

2. The coin had Caesar's name on it. If you are a Christian, what name is on you?

_____

Make a Picture Frame to Say You Belong to God

What You Need

- two 3" x 5" cards and a stand (use the pattern)
- photo of you
- ruler
- pencil
- scissors
- tape
- 3" x 5" piece of clear plastic (such as from a report cover)
- glue

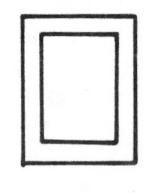

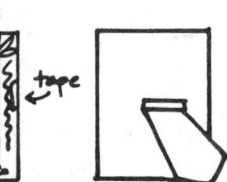

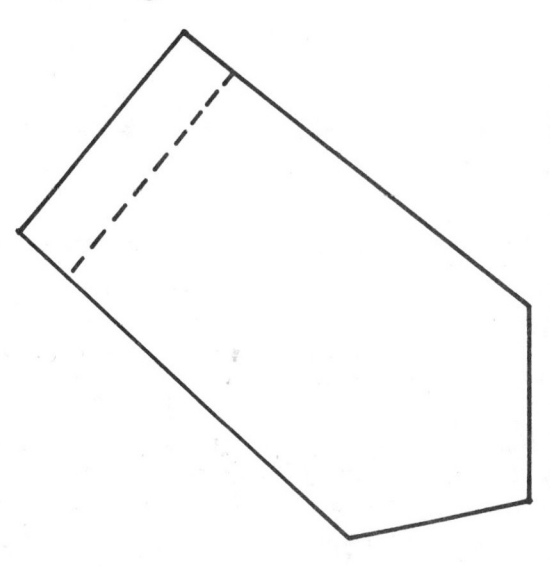

What You Do

1. Draw a rectangle 3/4 inch inside the edges of the 3" x 5" card that will be the front of the frame. Cut it out.
2. Write "I belong to God" across the bottom of the frame front.
3. Color a design around the front of the frame.
4. Lay the frame on top of the plastic piece and then lay these on top of the uncut card. Tape these together on the top and sides, leaving the bottom untaped.
5. Slide in photo between the plastic and the back of the frame. If it won't fit, trim a little off the edges.
6. Bend the stand. Glue the top part of the stand to the back of the frame as shown. Let it dry.

Draw a star in this box when you've read Matthew 22:15-22; Mark 12:13-17; Luke 20:19-26.

I DID IT!

Life and Lessons of Jesus Series

COMPLETED		DATE	COMPLETED		DATE
☐	The Work God Wants	_____	☐	Make Clothespin Puppets	_____
☐	Keep the Faith	_____	☐	The Rich Young Man	_____
☐	Love with All Your Heart	_____	☐	Choose Your Master	_____
☐	Be Born Again	_____	☐	Store Treasure in Heaven	_____
☐	My Birth Announcements	_____	☐	Serve God with Money	_____
☐	Join the Family	_____	☐	Be Sincere	_____
☐	Get on the Narrow Road	_____	☐	Right Reasons	_____
☐	The Old and the New	_____	☐	Produce Good Fruit	_____
☐	Build Your House on the Rock	_____	☐	Good Ground	_____
☐	Love Each Other	_____	☐	Be Careful Who You Follow	_____
☐	Tell the Good News	_____	☐	Be Sure It's in the Bible	_____
☐	Make a T-Shirt to Help with the Harvest	_____	☐	Remember What's Important	_____
☐	Jesus' Overpaid Workers	_____	☐	Daily Planner	_____
☐	Let Your Light Shine	_____	☐	Keep Your Good Deeds Secret	_____
☐	A Bright Reminder	_____	☐	Get Rid of What Causes Sin	_____
☐	Be Salty	_____	☐	Count the Cost	_____
☐	The Prodigal Son	_____	☐	Don't Look Back	_____
☐	Help the Poor	_____	☐	Give God What Is His	_____

ANSWERS

Page 5   Believe in Jesus
He who stands firm to the end will be saved.

Page 10   **Enter** through the narrow **gate**. For wide is the gate and broad is the road that leads to destruction, and many enter through it. But small is the gate and **narrow** the road that leads to **life**, and only a **few** find it.

Page 11   Jesus didn't come to patch up or add to the old ways (the law). He came to bring a new way (grace).

Page 14   Bad News: None of us deserve to live with God because we have all sinned.
Good News: If we have faith in Jesus, our sins are forgiven and we will live with God.

Page 17   God's grace is more than anyone deserves, and He gives it the same to all who enter His kingdom.

Page 18   Brighten the world around you by letting people see Jesus in you.

Page 19   1. Give a big smile; 2. Tell about Jesus; 3. Offer to help people; 4. Forgive others

Page 21

Page 22

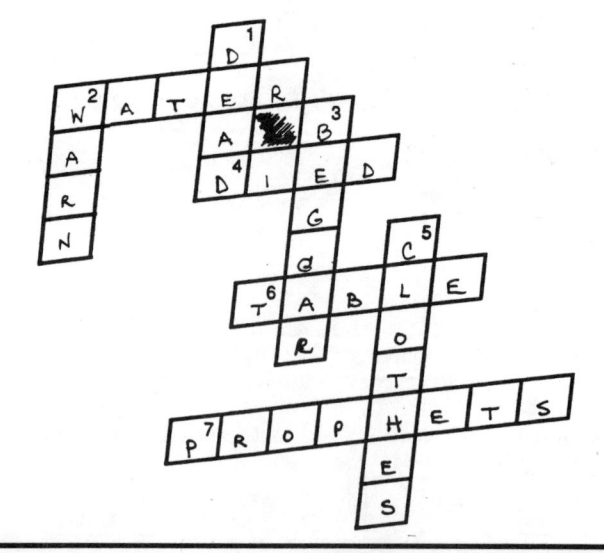

ANSWERS

Page 24   I will serve God with my money.

Page 25   You cannot serve both God and money.

Page 26   Your heart will be where your treasure is.

Page 27   1. Some feel they do not need God. 2. Some think they are better than other people. 3. Some will not share with others. 4. Some do not let God use their money how He wants.

Page 28   Camels: You obey picky little laws but disobey God in big ways.
Dishes: To be truly good, people must have their hearts changed by Jesus.
Bones: They did not believe in Jesus.

Page 29   Anything you hide will be shown later. What you say in the dark will be heard in the daylight. What you whisper in your room will be yelled from the roof.

Page 30

Page 31   1-A; 2-C; 3-D; 4-B

Page 32   If a blind man leads a blind man, both will fall into a pit.

Page 33   Bear - yes; Hen - yes; Elephant - no; Goat - yes; Kangaroo - no; Lion - yes

Page 34   Do not be too busy to learn from the Lord.

Page 37   What do I need to get rid of to keep from sinning?

Page 38   14 marshmallows; 25 toothpicks

Page 39   Decide to serve Jesus and then don't slow down or stop. Don't ever think about going back to the life you had before you asked Jesus to be your Lord.

Page 40   1. People; 2. God's

Index of *The Life and Lessons of Jesus* Series

BOOKS

1. Jesus Is Born
2. Jesus Grows Up
3. Jesus Prepares to Serve
4. Jesus Works Miracles
5. Jesus Heals
6. Learning to Love Like Jesus
7. Jesus Teaches Me to Pray
8. Following Jesus
9. Jesus Shows God's Love
10. Names of Jesus
11. Jesus' Last Week
12. Jesus Is Alive!

BIBLE STORY	LIFE AND LESSONS	BIBLE STORY	LIFE AND LESSONS
1st Miraculous Catch of Fish	Book 4	Great Commission	Book 12
2nd Miraculous Catch of Fish	Books 4, 12	Greatest Commandments	Books 6, 8
10 Disciples See Jesus	Book 12	Greatest Is Servant	Book 6
Angels Visit Shepherds	Book 1	Hairs Are Numbered	Book 9
As Father Has Loved Me . . .	Books 9, 11	Hand on Plow	Book 8
Ascension	Book 12	Healing at the Pool of Bethesda	Book 5
Ask in Jesus' Name	Book 11	Healing of 10 Lepers	Book 5
Ask, Seek, Knock	Book 7	Healing of a Blind Man	Book 6
		Healing of a Deaf and Mute Man	Book 6
Baby Jesus at the Temple	Book 2	Healing of a Leper	Book 5
Baptism of Jesus	Book 3	Healing of a Man's Hand	Book 5
Beatitudes	Books 6, 9	Healing of Blind Bartimaeus	Book 5
Becoming Child of God	Book 9	Healing of Centurion's Servant	Book 5
Belief and Baptism	Books 8, 12	Healing of Epileptic Boy	Book 5
Blind Leading Blind	Book 8	Healing of Malchus's Ear	Book 5
Boy Jesus at the Temple	Books 2, 3	Healing of Man Born Blind	Book 6
		Healing of Man with Dropsy	Book 5
Calming the Storm	Book 4	Healing of Official's Son	Book 5
Careless Words	Book 6	Healing of Peter's Mother-in-Law	Book 5
Christian Christmas Ideas	Book 1	Healing of the Paralytic	Book 5
Christian Easter Story and Activities	Books 11, 12	Healing of the Woman's Back	Book 5
Coin in Fish's Mouth	Book 4	Healing of Woman Who Touched Hem	Book 5
Count the Cost	Book 8	Heaven	Book 12
		How Much God Loves Us	Book 9
Demons into Pigs	Book 5	Humble Prayer	Book 7
Disciples Find a Donkey	Book 11		
Divorce/Stay Married	Book 6	I Am with You Always	Book 12
Do Not Let Your Heart Be Troubled	Book 11	I Live/You Will Live	Book 11
Don't Insult Others	Book 6	Include Others	Book 6
Don't Worry About Food and Clothes	Books 7, 9		
		Jesus Clears the Temple	Book 11
Endure to the End	Book 8	Jesus Died for Me	Book 9
Escape to Egypt	Book 2	Jesus Eats with Sinners	Book 9
Extra Mile	Book 6	Jesus Has Overcome the World	Book 11
		Jesus Is 'I AM'	Book 10
Faith of a Mustard Seed	Book 7	Jesus Is Arrested	Book 11
Faith to Move a Mountain	Book 7	Jesus Is Born	Books 1, 2
Fasting	Book 7	Jesus Is Buried	Book 11
Feed My Sheep	Book 12	Jesus Is Christ	Books 3, 10
Feeding the 5,000 and 4,000	Book 4	Jesus Is Crucified and Dies	Book 11
Forgive	Books 6, 7	Jesus Is God	Book 10
Forgiven Much, Love Much	Book 9	Jesus Is Immanuel	Book 10
		Jesus Is Tempted	Book 3
Gabriel Visits Mary	Book 1	Jesus Is the Bread of Life	Book 10
Garden of Gethsemane	Book 11	Jesus Is the Bridegroom	Book 10
Get Rid of What Causes Sin	Book 8	Jesus Is the Chief Cornerstone	Book 10
Gift of Holy Spirit	Books 9, 12	Jesus Is the Gate	Book 10
Give and Lend	Book 6	Jesus Is the Gift of God	Book 10
Give to Caesar What Is Caesar's	Book 8	Jesus Is the Good Shepherd	Book 10
God and Money	Book 8	Jesus Is the Lamb of God	Book 10
God Gives Good Gifts	Book 7	Jesus Is the Light	Book 10
God Wants Us in Heaven	Book 9	Jesus Is the Redeemer	Book 10
Golden Rule	Book 6	Jesus Is the Resurrection and Life	Book 10
Good Deeds in Secret	Book 8	Jesus Is the Savior	Book 10

Index of *The Life and Lessons of Jesus* Series

BIBLE STORY	LIFE AND LESSONS	BIBLE STORY	LIFE AND LESSONS
Jesus Is the Son of God	Book 10	Parable of the Unforgiving Servant	Book 6
Jesus Is the Truth	Book 10	Parable of Wedding Feast	Book 10
Jesus Is the Vine	Book 10	Parable of Weeds	Book 12
Jesus Is the Way	Books 10, 11	Parable of Wise and Foolish Builders	Book 10
Jesus Is the Word	Book 10	Parables of Mustard Seed and Leaven	Books 10, 12
Jesus Loves Children	Book 9	Parables of Treasure, Pearl, Fishnet	Books 10, 12
Jesus Obeys Parents	Book 2	Passover	Books 2, 10, 11
Jesus Prayed	Book 7	Peter's Denial	Books 3, 11
Jesus Shows Compassion	Book 9	Pharisee and Tax Collector at Temple	Book 6
Jesus Washes Disciples' Feet	Books 6, 10, 11	Pharisees' Hypocrisy	Book 8
Jesus' Family	Book 2	Pray Always	Book 7
Jesus' Genealogy	Book 1	Prepare a Place for You	Books 9, 11, 12
Jesus' Trial Before Caiaphas	Book 11	Promise of Holy Spirit	Book 11
Jesus' Trial Before Pilate	Book 11		
John the Baptist	Book 3	Raising of Jairus's Daughter	Book 5
Joseph's Dream	Book 1	Raising of Lazarus	Book 5
Judas Betrays Jesus	Books 3, 11	Raising of Widow's Son	Book 5
Judge Not	Book 6	Rich Toward God	Book 8
		Rich Young Ruler	Book 8
Known by Fruits	Book 8	Road to Emmaus	Book 12
Last Supper	Book 11	Salt of the Earth	Book 8
Lay Down Life for Friends	Books 8, 10, 11	Second Coming	Book 12
Lazarus and the Rich Man	Book 8	Seek Kingdom First	Book 7
Life in New Testament Times	Book 2	Seventy Times Seven	Book 6
Light on a Hill	Book 8	Sheep Know His Voice	Book 7
Like Days of Noah	Book 12	Shepherd Knows Sheep	Book 9
Like Jonah's Three Days in Fish	Book 12	Speck and the Plank	Book 6
Lord's Prayer	Book 7	Spiritual Harvest	Book 8
Love Each Other	Book 11		
Love Jesus Most	Book 9	Take Up Your Cross	Book 9
Love Me/Obey Me	Book 11	Thief in the Night	Book 12
Love One Another	Book 8	Thomas Sees Resurrected Jesus	Book 12
Loving Enemies	Books 6, 7	Transfiguration	Book 3
		Treasure in Heaven	Book 8
Make Up Quickly	Book 6	Triumphal Entry	Book 11
Maps of New Testament Times	Books 1-5	True Members of Jesus' Family	Book 2
Mary and Martha	Book 8	Truth Makes You Free	Book 10
Mary Anoints Jesus with Perfume	Book 11	Twelve Disciples	Book 3
Mary Visits Elizabeth	Book 1	Two Agree in Prayer	Book 7
Name the Baby Jesus	Book 10	Under His Wing	Book 9
Narrow Road	Book 8		
New Commandment: Love	Book 6	Vine and Branches	Book 10
Nicodemus	Book 8		
Not Left As Orphans	Book 11	Walking on Water	Book 4
		Water to Wine	Book 4
Old and New Cloth	Book 8	What Makes a Person Unclean	Book 8
Oxen in a Pit	Book 5	Widow's Mites	Book 8
		Wine and Wineskins	Book 8
Parable of the Friend at Midnight	Book 7	Wise Men Visit Jesus	Book 1
Parable of the Good Samaritan	Book 6	Withered Fig Tree	Book 4
Parable of the Lost Coin	Book 9	Wolves in Sheep's Clothing	Book 8
Parable of the Lost Sheep	Book 9	Woman at the Well	Book 10
Parable of the Overpaid Workers	Book 8	Woman Caught Sinning	Book 6
Parable of the Persistent Widow	Book 7	Worth More than Sparrows	Book 9
Parable of the Prodigal Son	Books 7, 8		
Parable of the Sheep and Goats	Books 6, 12	Yoke Easy, Burden Light	Book 7
Parable of Sower and Seeds	Books 8, 10, 12		
Parable of the Ten Young Women	Book 10	Zaccheus	Book 9

If you would like to write to the author, send your letter to:

Your address here

Stamp here

Tracy L. Harrast
c/o Church Resources Dept.
David C. Cook Publishing Co.
850 N. Grove Avenue
Elgin, IL 60120